PIRATES AROUND THE WORLD
Terror on the High Seas

Blackbeard
(Edward Teach)

Tammy Gagne

Mitchell Lane
PUBLISHERS
P.O. Box 196
Hockessin, DE 19707
www.mitchelllane.com

PUBLISHERS

Printing   1   2   3   4   5   6   7   8

Anne Bonny

Black Bart (Bartholomew Roberts)

Blackbeard (Edward Teach)

François L'Olonnais

Long Ben (Henry Every)

Sir Francis Drake

Sir Henry Morgan

William Kidd

Library of Congress Cataloging-in-Publication Data
Gagne, Tammy.
  Blackbeard (Edward Teach) / by Tammy Gagne.
    pages cm. — (Pirates Around the World: Terror on the High Seas)
  Includes webography.
  Includes bibliographical references and index.
  Audience: Age: 8 to 11.
  Audience: Grade: 3 to 6.
  ISBN 978-1-68020-036-2 (library bound)
  1. Teach, Edward, -1718—Juvenile literature. 2. Pirates—Biography—Juvenile literature. I. Title.
  G537.T4G34 2015
  910.4'5—dc23
  [B]
                                                                    2015017148

eBook ISBN: 978-1-68020-037-9

PUBLISHER'S NOTE: The Internet sites referenced herein were active as of the publication date. Due to the fleeting nature of some web sites, we cannot guarantee they will all be active when you are reading this book.

Contents

Words in **bold** throughout can be found in the Glossary.

Edward Teach, better known as Blackbeard, went down in history as a fearsome pirate of the 18th century. Stories about Blackbeard and his violent ways spread quickly from the Caribbean islands all the way to the New England colonies. No one knew how many of the tales were true. And no one wanted to find out.

The Most Feared Pirate

For Michael and Doris Daniels of New York City, their favorite family campground at Ocracoke, just south of Cape Hatteras on the Outer Banks of North Carolina, offered a peaceful view of the Atlantic Ocean. But for their children, Logan and Isabella, the beach had been transformed into a pirates' den. The picnic table where they had just eaten dinner was now the deck of a magnificent pirate ship with billowing sails and dozens of cannon. Logan had made a skull and crossbones flag from construction-paper that blew in the salty breeze. It was an unmistakable warning: Everyone in their path was in terrible peril.

"I'm Captain Jack Sparrow!" Isabella announced to her brother. She wore a red bandana covering her hair and sported one of her mother's gold hoop earrings. Being the younger sister, Isabella usually got stuck playing second fiddle. But this time she was certain she had called the best pirate first. Honestly, though, she didn't know of any others.

"You can be Jack Sparrow if you want, Izzy," Logan answered her. "But you know he wasn't a real person, right? Jack Sparrow was based on Bartholomew Roberts. People called him Black Bart." Isabella became worried. Was Logan bluffing to get her to give up the best pirate role so he could play the part himself? Before she could decide,

5

her older brother added, "I'm going to be Blackbeard. He was real."

"Were there any other real pirates?," she asked.

"Of course," Logan replied, pleased to show off his knowledge about **swashbucklers**. "There was Calico Jack, Sir Francis Drake, William Kidd and Blackbeard. His real name was Edward Teach. He was the most famous pirate of them all."

"Why?," his little sister asked. Isabella's never-ending questions usually drove Logan mad. But he didn't mind explaining this particular subject to her.

"According to legend, Blackbeard was the most feared pirate in the entire Caribbean and along the Atlantic coast," Logan began. "He struck terror in the hearts of all who saw him." He'd read that last part in one of his library books. "The people he attacked would shake in their boots just at the sight of him!"

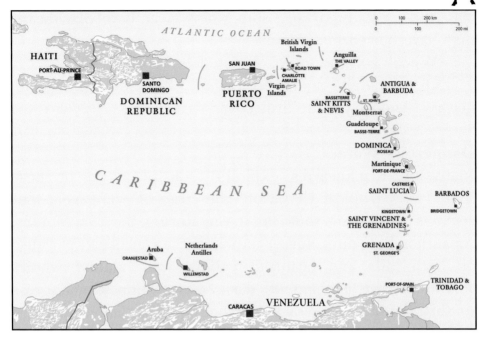

The island of Trinidad is located just off the coast of Venezuela. During the 18th century, Trinidad was not an easy place for ships to reach. This fact made the beautiful landmass the perfect home away from home for a pirate like Blackbeard.

"And most important, somewhere near here Blackbeard may have buried his treasure."

"Whoa! Tell me more!" insisted Isabella.

"Okay, matey," answered Logan. "Let's dig into pirate history. And maybe we'll discover treasure."

Dangerous Waters

Many of Blackbeard's exploits took place on or near Trinidad, a tropical island off the coast of Venezuela that remains as alluring today as it was during the 18th century. As author Benjamin Barker explains, the Caribbean paradise of high hills and beautiful valleys was "almost wholly surrounded by a chain of dark, rocky cliffs, which gives to this remote island a somewhat fantastic appearance to the eye of the beholder, as he approaches it from the sea."[1] Only a single small beach on the island's southern side was protected enough for a boat to drop anchor near land.

As difficult as the island was to reach, many Spaniards set sail for the distant colony. Some suffering from poor health hoped the Caribbean isle's tropical climate would restore their vigor. Many of the plants growing on Trinidad were said to possess healing properties. But those sailing there often paid a dear price. Many ships never made it across the Atlantic. And the ones that did often encountered pirates.

A Scary Sight

Barker describes Blackbeard as tall and ferocious. The pirate dressed in distinctive clothing that set him apart. He wore "loose Turkish trousers of crimson silk" and a long shirt of the same colorful fabric. The outfit was wrapped with a sash that also held "a large pair of pistols and a small Spanish **stiletto** of the most costly workmanship." From under a red cap, notes Barker, "a mass of long black

Drawings of Blackbeard show him as a scary-looking man with long hair and the beard for which he received his nickname. This piece is called "The Quest for Pirates' Gold." It depicts Blackbeard with his crew as they prepare for an attack, weapons in hand. It may or may not show what Teach actually looked like, though. The drawing was published a century after his famous raids took place.

hair" spilled out, nearly covering his face.[2] And then, there was the bushy beard for which Blackbeard was named. The combination of untamed hair and deadly weapons gave him a menacing look.

Blackbeard wanted people to fear him greatly. The pirate reportedly would set his hair on fire before battle to make his appearance even more terrifying. Another explanation is that he lit lengths of hemp rope dipped in lime and saltpeter which he positioned under his hat. The flames and smoke gave his face a fierce glow.

Many of the 45 or so vessels Blackbeard seized between 1713 and 1718 surrendered without resistance as soon as he approached. When anyone refused his demands, the pirate

didn't hesitate to show just how cruel he could be. People who hesitated to turn over their valuable rings, for example, would have their fingers chopped off.

Ships that tried to flee from Blackbeard and his crew stood little chance of getting away. He commanded a 40-gun warship he called *Queen Anne's Revenge.* His crew was made up of fierce men who, like the pirate captain himself, were ruthless in their pursuit of treasure. But even the boldest crew members knew better than to cross their captain. In order to keep his pirate crew in line, it is said that Blackbeard would sometimes kill one of them—just to remind the others who was in charge.

A model of Blackbeard's **Queen Anne's Revenge** *is on display at the North Carolina Maritime Museum.*

An Image More Frightening Than the Man Himself

While Blackbeard was one of the best known pirates of the 18th century, many of the details about his career are inaccurate, starting with his name. Smithsonian.com journalist Colin Woodard points out, "He went by Edward Thatch—not 'Teach' as many historians have said, apparently repeating an error made by the *Boston News-Letter*."[3]

Kevin Duffus, author of *The Last Days of Blackbeard the Pirate*, disputes the story about Blackbeard's burning hair. "Based on the historic record, none of that is true," Duffus stated in an interview. "There is only one single authoritative source that describes Blackbeard's appearance, and it was just a few short words. He was a tall, spare man with a beard that he wore very long. And that's it."[4]

Tales of Blackbeard's bloodthirstiness are also questionable. In 2008, Trent University historian Arne Bialuschewski uncovered a cache of dozens of firsthand accounts of the pirate in an archive in Jamaica. Bear in mind these statements were written by people whom Blackbeard had taken prisoner. "I haven't seen one single piece of evidence that Blackbeard ever used violence against anyone," Bialuschewski shares.[5]

Blackbeard was a successful pirate. But the historian believes that it was later storytellers who transformed him into a fearsome legend.

Bahamas Blackbeard Pirate Stamp

Spain's King Philip V was the grandson of a French monarch. He assumed the throne when Spain's King Charles II passed away without any heirs. The decision to name a Frenchman as king of Spain triggered a global conflict, called the War of Spanish Succession. In North America, where the global battle was called Queen Anne's War, piracy became a form of economic warfare.

From Privateering to Piracy

When Spain's King Charles II died in 1700, he had no heir to assume the monarchy. Charles willed his earthly possessions to Philip, the Duke of Anjou, who was the grandson of France's King Louis XIV. France quickly claimed the empty throne. But Britain, the Netherlands and several other European countries thought that a joint French-Spanish king would make the united countries too powerful. The resulting conflict led to the War of Spanish Succession that began in 1701 and continued until 1714. In North America, the global battle was called Queen Anne's War.

A Pirate's Life for Him

Most historians concur that Edward Teach was born around 1680 in Bristol, England. Fate had it that he would become a pirate. In his youth, he went to sea for his country during the war for the Spanish throne. He served as a **privateer**, a mercenary armed with a **letter of marque and reprisal**, which made him a legalized pirate during times of war. From hidden bays privateers like him set out to attack heavily laden, and often defenseless, merchant ships leaving the Spanish Main. When privateers took control of an enemy ship, they would claim her and all the supplies and maps aboard for their country. In place of a salary, privateers were allowed to keep most of the enemy property they seized.

The only difference between the work of privateers and that of pirates was that the former profession was permitted by law. It's no wonder then that Teach would become a pirate when the Spanish war came to an end. After all, his country had taught him how to make a handsome living by grand theft at sea.

The War of Spanish Succession took Teach to the Caribbean. There, he raided cargo **galleons** as they sailed to and from Spanish colonies like Trinidad, Nueva España (Mexico) meaning New Spain, and Peru.

A Quick Study

In 1713 Teach graduated from privateer to pirate, becoming a crewman in a Jamaican sloop under the command of Captain Benjamin Thornigold, sometimes written as Hornigold. This pirate captain, sailing out of the island of New Providence in the Bahamas, did not confine his pillaging to the Caribbean, however—nor to Spanish ships.

Old Spanish galleon in Genoa harbor

"He raided vessels on both sides of the Atlantic and belonging to all nationalities," wrote Carl Goerch in his 1956 book *Ocracoke.*[1]

Goerch reported that Teach quickly became fascinated by his new profession. "He showed so much interest and demonstrated so much enthusiasm and energy that he soon became Thornigold's chief lieutenant."[2] By 1717, the captain began allowing Teach to make voyages of his own. But Thornigold and his **protégé** had a falling out. In 1718 Thornigold turned pirate hunter and pursued his former allies on behalf of the Governor of the Bahamas. He was killed in 1719 when his ship was wrecked on a reef during the hurricane season.

Working for Thornigold, Teach sailed to Britain's colonies along the Atlantic coast of North America. "Teach was in his element," wrote Goerch. "He enjoyed the fighting and appreciated the **plunder**. It wasn't long before he was recognized as a chief of the pirates, ranking even ahead of Thornigold."[3] When the senior pirate quit piracy altogether, he gave Teach the French merchant vessel that they had captured together. Called *La Concorde de Nantes*, the frigate was fitted to carry slaves from Africa. It had been launched in 1710 as the Royal Navy's HMS *Concord*. Teach made the vessel his flagship, renamed her *Queen Anne's Revenge* and doubled her firepower to forty cannon.

One of Teach's solo expeditions took him just outside the port of Charleston, South Carolina, then known as Charles Town. There Blackbeard, as he was now known, waited patiently for a ship approaching or leaving the bustling harbor. As expected, a vessel bound for London soon appeared. The talented pirate and his crew easily captured her. Soon three additional smaller vessels followed. Teach and his men seized them all.

Capturing a ship was nothing new to Teach. But this time he was after more than the usual supplies of flour or rum, or even gold. An ailing crewmate was in need of medicine. Teach knew just how he was going to get it. He immediately freed a number of British sailors. He likely wanted them to spread the word of their capture. Nothing,

Few sailors could triumph over Blackbeard and his crew.

after all, would be as effective at striking fear in the hearts of the colonists as a firsthand report of being captured by pirates. Blackbeard kept several of the better-known citizens aboard the ship as **hostages**. They were the key to getting the drugs he needed.

Teach sent two of his lieutenants to speak to Charles Eden, the colony's governor. The sailors swaggered through Charleston as if they owned the city. Pirates, particularly Teach, were known for their bold behavior. Meeting the governor, they informed him that if he wanted to save the hostages, he would have to provide a chest of medical supplies. Eden complied, and Teach released the prisoners, as promised. But first he made sure to strip them of everything of value.

Teach quickly discovered that the Atlantic coastline of the American colonies offered a gold mine for pirates. Stretching 2,000 miles from Maine to South Carolina, the seaboard was lined with busy harbors. The goods that passed through these ports were what made **civilized** life pleasant in the remote New World. But Teach didn't have to be civil or abide by laws. Sailors and shipping masters alike feared him. Blackbeard's reputation as a treacherous pirate spread quickly.

Not Far from Home at All

Many of the "facts" and myths about Blackbeard are questionable. According to historian Kevin Duffus, the pirate was born in the New World rather than in England. "It is my opinion that Edward 'Black' Beard, son of Captain James Beard, was likely born at Goose Creek sometime around 1690." This North Carolina town isn't far from Charleston, where Blackbeard took his hostages and received his medicines.

"Traditional historical accounts have suggested that Black Beard was born in 1680," adds Duffus, "which would have made him 38 at the time of his death. That would have made him a rather old pirate."[4]

Journalist Brian Hicks offers, "Duffus' theory centers on a man who lived in Bath Town, N.C., in 1706 named Capt. James Beard. A trio of genealogists traced the man's trail backward to Charleston and Barbados. Beard lived on the Cooper River in what is now Goose Creek, South Carolina before moving to North Carolina. In his will, he left his property to an unnamed son."[5] Another convincing fact that supports the theory comes from the property tax records. The unnamed son paid taxes on the property until 1718. No one has been able to prove that Blackbeard was indeed James Beard's son. But the pirate was killed that same year.

A map of Charleston in the 1700s.

British colonists feared sharing the Atlantic waters with Blackbeard and his crew. They didn't feel safe with the pirate on the loose. But their government did little to protect them from the known thief and his men.

Working Together?

As news about Blackbeard's piracy spread through the colonies, people began demanding that their local government do something to make the waters safer. They wanted the brigand stopped. But Governor Eden did nothing to capture the pirate. If anything, he made it easier for Blackbeard to continue his pillaging.

Friend in High Places

Remember that privateers kept only part of the loot they acquired from capturing enemy ships. Suspicions arose that Governor Eden was on the receiving end of a profit-sharing agreement with Blackbeard. Not that Eden needed more wealth. He already owned a 400-acre plantation on the banks of Bath Creek. But wealth does not necessarily erase greed. Some even say that the governor ordered a hidden passage be built into his mansion's cellar. By traveling through this secret doorway, Blackbeard and the governor could meet without being seen.

What damaged Eden's standing even more were the official acts he performed for the pirate. As an agent of His Majesty's government, Governor Eden bestowed a royal pardon on Blackbeard in 1718. This set aside any punishment the pirate might have received for his crimes. Eden also helped Blackbeard with another legal—but more

personal—matter. While the pirate was in North Carolina, a 16-year-old beauty caught his eye. Having the authority to perform civil marriages, Governor Eden officiated at the pair's wedding. The teenage colonist became the pirate's fourteenth wife. In total, Blackbeard fathered forty children.

Having a new bride did not keep Blackbeard on dry land, however. He continued pillaging up and down the Atlantic coast, seizing whatever he could. He also returned to the Caribbean. In 1717, near the island of St. Vincent, he brought down his biggest prize yet—literally. Called the *Great Allen*, the vessel could have become his own. But instead, the pirate removed all of her supplies before burning and sinking her.

Leading with Fear

Of course, no one could accomplish a feat like this one alone. Blackbeard's crew was an essential part of his success. Training hundreds of men to be fearless and loyal was not an easy task. But then, Blackbeard was no ordinary pirate. He ran a tight ship with strict rules. Yes, even pirates had regulations.

The most important quality of a pirate was bravery. If his men backed down in the face of danger, an enemy boat might escape. To prevent this from happening, Blackbeard killed some of his sailors whom he accused of cowardice. One form of capital punishment was "walking the plank."

Another favorite punishment was to **maroon** a rule-breaker on a tiny, uninhabited isle. If Blackbeard was feeling merciful, he might leave the abandoned crew member a bottle of water and a pistol loaded with a single shot. Many used that weapon to end their starvation and suffering.

Crew members found guilty of lesser offenses would be forced to endure other brutal punishments such

Blackbeard kept his men loyal by making them fear him. If they showed the least amount of disrespect, he would flog or whip them for their behavior. Others suffered much worse fates.

as **flogging**. The guilty party would bare his back and receive lashes from a whip of nine knotted rope cords called a cat o'nine tails.

Fights between crew members were handled differently. The men would be sent ashore for a duel. Blackbeard did not have to decide who was guilty. Whoever survived would be the victor. Duels, like walking the plank, also served as entertainment for crew members accustomed to such violence.

The Pirate Business

When many people think of pirates, they picture wooden chests overflowing with gold and silver bars mined in Spain's New World colonies. Certainly, Blackbeard and other Caribbean pirates acquired their share of this

Crew members whom Blackbeard marooned on islands had little hope of surviving the ordeal.

traditional loot. Legends state that Blackbeard buried some of it in a secret location. But the majority of the treasure that these 18th century pirates stole consisted of more practical goods. People living in the colonies needed supplies such as textiles. Merchant ships from Great Britain usually carried these useful items. Ships from the Caribbean often brought cocoa and sugar while boats from Africa brought slaves.

Blackbeard and his crew could never have used all the trade goods that they stole from the ships they raided. In order to make his efforts worthwhile, the pirate had to sell most of the goods. This is where everyday colonists come into the story. It was they, after all, who bought many of the stolen items the pirate offered for sale.

Buying stolen goods was illegal. "Still, the local townspeople tolerated Blackbeard because they liked to buy the goods he stole, which were cheaper than imported English goods," writes journalist Stefan Lovgren.[1] For everyday people, Blackbeard's goods were bargains. Sailors may have feared him. But many people were willing to look the other way if it meant saving money.

Based on the True Story

Over time much fiction has been written about Blackbeard. But we cannot simply dismiss the stories about him as lies. These legends are a mixture of truth and exaggeration. No one knows for certain whether Governor Eden was in business with Blackbeard. The story about the secret passage, for example, may have been created by people who visited Eden's home. The North Carolina Historic Sites' website states, "Such a tunnel probably never existed but there was a path of ballast rocks that led from Eden's place to a pier on the creek nearby."[2]

This is not to say that no British officials helped Blackbeard commit his crimes. A man named Tobias Knight was secretary of the colony. He owned the plantation next to Eden's. "It was Knight's house that stood on what is now known as Archbell Point," notes the North Carolina Historic Sites. "And it was Knight—not Governor Eden—who was later tried before Council for being an accessory to piratical acts associated with Blackbeard and his crew."[3]

But why, you may ask, would Eden perform a marriage ceremony for the pirate? The North Carolina Historic Sites website addresses this question as well. "[T]his incident has been suggested as proof that the pirate and the governor were friends allied in the commission of piratical acts. In all probability, however, Eden was the only official in the area who could legally perform such ceremonies."[4]

Many North Carolina plantations of Blackbeard's era were large and extravagant places. It is easy to see how the pirate could have been lining the pockets of the owners.

Gold and silver weren't the only items that Blackbeard stole. Being a pirate meant stealing anything of value—from textiles to tobacco. It therefore also meant having to sell off all these goods.

Governor Spotswood to the Rescue

Blackbeard created a successful if criminal business for himself. But it could only work as long as people either feared him or worked with him. Even if Governor Eden did not help the pirate, he and his fellow North Carolinians surely didn't try very hard to stop him. The same could not be said for the next colony to the north, though. Virginia Governor Alexander Spotswood was fed up with Blackbeard and his assaults on the ships sailing in and out of his colony's harbors.

Blackbeard had shut down much of Virginia's trade. The entrance to Chesapeake Bay between Cape Henry and Cape Charles, for instance, was closed for weeks at a time because of the threat of pirate's raids. In just two years, Blackbeard successfully attacked some 45 ships in the Atlantic and Caribbean. He was no longer just a pirate. He had become the symbol of piracy.

The tide against pirates turned in 1718 when Woodes Rogers was appointed governor of the Bahamas. Like Blackbeard, he had been a privateer in Britain's Royal Navy. This experience gave him an important advantage. Empowered by King George I, Rogers offered all pirates a deal. If they immediately surrendered, he promised a royal pardon. It was an easy way out for those tired of their dangerous profession. Rogers vowed to hunt down all

pirates who passed up the deal, offering no mercy to those he captured.

Rogers' offer of amnesty marked the beginning of the end of piracy in the Caribbean in the 18th century. But the situation to the north would get worse before it got better. While half of the pirates accepted the amnesty and retired, the other half traveled up the Atlantic coast, where they raided ships off the coast of the American colonies.

Virginia was an ideal target for Blackbeard and the remaining pirates. The colony had many ports that it used for exporting tobacco. These harbors were situated around numerous capes. These jutting headlands offered excellent hiding spots for pirates. The thieves could wait patiently in a quiet cove, unseen until the moment they attacked.

Historian John V. Quarstein adds Blackbeard was well prepared to follow through once he began his raids. "His ship—the *Queen Anne's Revenge*—also was one of the most powerful pirate vessels and one of the most powerful ships in American waters at the time. So it's no surprise that Charleston and the whole East Coast were so fearful." He didn't just take on one ship at a time. When he showed up in North Carolina, for instance, "Blackbeard captured and plundered every ship that passed by for a week. . . ."[1]

As colonists were buying the pirate's goods, North Carolina merchants were pleading for help from their local government. When no one answered their calls in their own colony, they turned to the neighboring governor. Perhaps Spotswood could accomplish what Eden could not—or would not—do.

The Virginia governor realized that the key to stopping people from buying Blackbeard's goods was to offer them something better. He extended a generous reward for the capture of the pirate, his men, and their ship. He didn't really think that an everyday colonist would stop Blackbeard. But the possibility proved to be an effective incentive to refuse discounted stolen goods.

Meanwhile, Spotswood sent two Royal Navy battleships to stop Blackbeard once and for all. He placed a lieutenant named Robert Maynard in charge of the critical assignment. According to journalist Gregory Elder, "Maynard spotted Blackbeard's vessel off the coast of North Carolina, and moved in close for a kill. But Maynard's ships had few guns, and Blackbeard fired several deadly shots into the hulls of the Royal Navy vessels. But the royal vessel bore in hard and forced Blackbeard's ship onto a sandbar." Still, the determined pirate would not give up. "Blackbeard ordered his men to throw everything overboard and managed to get his ship afloat again."[2]

Thankfully for Spotswood, he had carefully chosen the leader of this mission. Blackbeard was stubborn. But Maynard was smarter. He sent most of his crew below decks and out of sight, hoping this would trick Blackbeard into thinking that his brigands outnumbered the Royal Navy attackers. Sometimes the simplest plans are the best. Falling for the ruse, the pirate and his men stormed aboard the ship. Before the pirates realized what was happening, Maynard's crew

Governor Alexander Spotswood

Blackbeard fell for Robert Maynard's trick when he boarded the Royal Navy's vessel. He assumed that he and his crew outnumbered Maynard and his men. The mistake would cost the pirate his life.

ambushed the greedy thieves, killing Blackbeard and many of his men.

"One account describes Maynard and Blackbeard shouting insults at one another as their forces engaged on the deck, and that the pirate paused for a refreshing glass of rum before entering the battle," writes Elder. He also notes that the pirate didn't go down easily. "[I]t took 20 stabs with sabers and five gunshot wounds to kill him."[3] When the battle was over, Maynard's crew beheaded Blackbeard. They tossed his decapitated body overboard but kept his head as proof that the pirate's reign of terror was over.

Another Flawed Hero

The stories about Blackbeard's capture have been told and retold for centuries. In most of them Spotswood is portrayed as a hero. While he played a key role in Blackbeard's demise, Spotswood himself was far from a respectable man. His own words only support his hero's status. "I thought it necessary to put a stop to the further progress of the robberies," the governor wrote.[4] But Colin Woodard reveals a man who also regularly broke the law.

"He didn't have the authority to send an expedition into another colony, but Spotswood was not one to be constrained by legal and ethical niceties. Legislators were already working to have him thrown out of office for various power grabs and for squandering tax revenue on Williamsburg's fantastically opulent new Governor's Palace. Through blind trusts he would ultimately give himself 85,000 acres of public land, an area that came to be known as Spotsylvania County."[5] Most of the stories about the Virginia governor fail to mention that his plan to eliminate the pirate was illegal, as it took place in North Carolina waters.

According to a gruesome legend, Blackbeard's headless body swam around his ship three times before finally sinking. While this would seem impossible, another part of the story is true. Woodard points out that Maynard and his men did indeed keep Blackbeard's severed head. It was "given as a trophy to Spotswood, who had it displayed on a tall pole in Hampton Roads, at a site now known as Blackbeard's Point."[6]

The Governor's Palace in Williamsburg, Virginia, completed by Alexander Spotswood and rebuilt in the 1930s.

Some legends about Blackbeard state that he buried some of the gold, silver, and jewels that he stole. No one knows for sure if this part of the story is true, however, or where the treasure might be.

Buried Treasure

The legend of Blackbeard, like his contemporary privateer and pirate Sir Henry Morgan, has survived to the present. People who study the pirate learn names like Eden and Spotswood. But good or bad, these men did not become nearly as famous as pirates. Even Maynard, who captured Blackbeard, is largely unknown. For a man whose career in piracy lasted less than five years, tales about Blackbeard have been going strong for three centuries.

One of the reasons has to do with Blackbeard's hidden treasure. As the legend goes, the pirate buried a large portion of the gold, silver and jewels that came into his possession. In 1718, before the last of his surviving crew members was hanged, the Royal Navy began searching for the pirate's buried loot. All the treasure hunters found were supplies and some letters.

Blackbeard never divulged any information about his treasure to his crew. Where exactly was it buried? How much was there? Where had he hidden it? Had he told his new wife? To these questions he simply replied, "Nobody knows but m'self and the Devil, and may the longest liver take all."[1]

Some people believe Blackbeard buried his treasure on Ocracoke Island, a sliver of land off the coast of North Carolina that was said to be Blackbeard's **lair**. Journalist

Joseph Cosco explains, "In Ocracoke, Blackbeard found a barren outpost strategically placed near North Carolina's major shipping lanes. All oceangoing vessels leaving or destined for settlements in northeastern North Carolina had to pass through Ocracoke Inlet, then the only gap in the string of barrier islands now called the Outer Banks. Blackbeard anchored at what has come to be known as Teach's Hole, on the sound side of the Ocracoke Island, near the southern end where the village sits today."[2]

In 1718, Blackbeard hosted a wild pirate party at his favorite hideout on the island. He and his crew danced, drank, and lit bonfires during the gathering, which lasted for days.

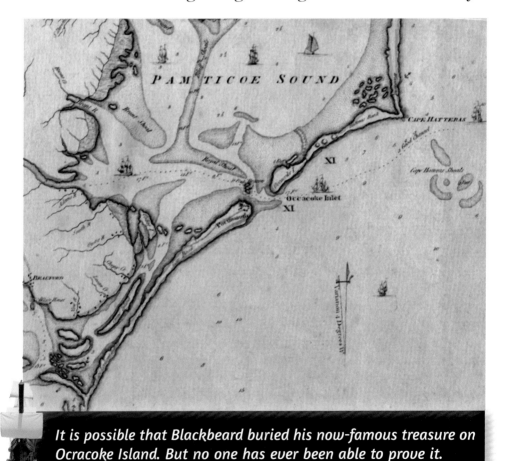

It is possible that Blackbeard buried his now-famous treasure on Ocracoke Island. But no one has ever been able to prove it.

Pirates from near and far sailed in to join the celebration. Legends say that it was this event that triggered Governor Spotswood's decision to end Blackbeard's piracy career. It was bad enough that the pirate was sailing into the colony's harbors and raiding British ships. But it was another thing entirely to set up camp on Crown land and rejoice in the spoils. Spotswood was determined not to let Blackbeard's fame grow any further.

Knowing that he might be confronted at any moment, the sly pirate may have hidden his most valuable loot somewhere on the 16-mile-long island. But the questions his crewman asked still linger. What did he bury? And where was it?

People who have studied Blackbeard call him a "master of psychological warfare."[3] His look and his over-the-top actions—it was all done to create the powerful persona he took on. Was he indeed a talented fighter? He certainly won many of the battles that he started. But he accomplished these feats largely by intimidation, "more often than not scaring the wits out of his prey without a fight."[4] Would such a cunning individual bury his treasure on an island that so many people linked to him?

Remember that Blackbeard began his piracy career in the Caribbean. And he sailed from there to the middle colonies many times. He could have buried his gold and other treasure anywhere along the way. Some have insisted that the pirate's booty is hidden in Florida. Others are sure that Blackbeard secreted it away somewhere in the Caribbean. And some think the treasure was buried at a site called the Money Pit on Oak Island, Nova Scotia, which was then part of the French colony of Acadia. Excavators there have found a Spanish coin from the 1600s.

CHAPTER 5

Many people have searched for Blackbeard's gold, silver, and jewels over the centuries. Some have dedicated years—and entire careers—to the goal. But so far none have located it. Perhaps more important, no one has been able to prove that it even exists. What keeps people looking, though, is the fact that no one has been able to prove that it doesn't exist either.

In 1996, however, another treasure of sorts was found. In shallow waters off the coast of North Carolina divers discovered the infamous *Queen Anne's Revenge*. For nearly 300 years, the wreck lay just 25 feet beneath the ocean's surface. If the pirate did keep his treasure on board, surely it would be part of the historic find.

But was the *Queen Anne's Revenge* even the ship that Blackbeard captained on that fateful day that Robert Maynard brought him and his vessel down? Some historians claim that it wasn't. Smithsonian.com journalist Abigail Tucker shares that some experts, "think Blackbeard deliberately abandoned the ship, which was far too large to navigate North Carolina's shallow sounds, in an effort to downsize his crew (some of whom later testified as much) and travel light, transferring his treasure to the smaller ships in his fleet. Whatever the scenario, the demise of the *Queen Anne's Revenge* was what marine archaeologists call a 'nonviolent wreck event,' meaning that the pirates had ample time to offload plunder."[5]

This information brings us right back where we started—with possibilities but no proof that any treasure was buried at all. A treasure map complete with that sought after X that marks the spot is a thrilling idea. But the information we know about Blackbeard tells us that he would never have created such a record. Clearly, he didn't want anyone to find what he had worked so hard to collect during his time as the most ruthless pirate of the Caribbean.

One Man's Treasure...

Whether you think that Blackbeard's treasure exists depends largely on your definition of treasure. Did the pirate bury gold and other precious items in a secret location? Maybe, maybe not. But are the items on his sunken ship worth as much as a **trove** of jewels would be? People who have been working to unearth these artifacts say yes.

Archeologists have continued to salvage items from the *Queen Anne's Revenge* since it was first discovered in 1996. Among them are cannons, anchors, and the dinner plates which Blackbeard and his crew ate off. Sitting on the ocean floor for so long has left many of these objects severely corroded and encrusted with salt. It can take as long as a decade to remove this patina so scientists can study the items.

"A treasure chest is an unlikely find in the wreckage," writes Jeremy A. Kaplan. "But what does exist, 300 years after the ship was abandoned in shallow waters, will be of incalculable value for future scholars. . . . There is navigation equipment, weaponry, ceramics, glass wear, personal effects, material from the African slave trade and more. These items are often locked in a concrete like crust of sand, shells and marine life that must be removed during the conservation process."[6]

The discovery of Blackbeard's ship has allowed archeologists to study items like this pewter flatware, likely used by the pirate and his crew.

Many different artists have depicted Edward Teach through the centuries. The images differ in small ways, but nearly all of them show Blackbeard as a larger-than-life villain. Surely, the artists drew on the wild stories about the pirate while making their creations.

The Truth within the Legend

The story of Blackbeard is undeniably a thrilling one that is best classified as a mystery. But one might also call many parts of it a fantasy. We know, of course, that Edward Teach—or Edward Thatch—was a real person. But much of what we think we know about his alter ego, Blackbeard, is almost certainly fiction. Could a headless body actually swim around a ship three times? Science tells us this is **preposterous**.

But many gray areas exist between the simple fact that Blackbeard was an actual person and the absurd idea that he was superhuman. Was he indeed a murderer or just very good at making people think that he was a merciless killer? At least some reputable sources are convinced that he wasn't just acting ruthlessly. *National Geographic* calls Blackbeard "the worst and perhaps the cruelest pirate of them all."[1]

It seems that the legends about Blackbeard, though, began with the pirate himself. A shrewd seafarer skilled in the art of thievery, he knew that the best weapon a pirate could have was fear. He began instilling fright in those who encountered him with his wild look. Civilized men of the early 18th century did not allow their hair—including facial hair—to grow as long as the pirate did. Just by looking different, he made himself stand out.

The matter of lighting his hair on fire served one of two purposes. Either his enemies would think Blackbeard was capable of supernatural feats, or they would think he was outright mad. The former scenario was definitely scarier. No sane person would want to engage in a battle with a pirate who could set his own hair on fire and live to fight another day. What kind of weapon would prove effective against such an entity, after all? And while a human being who would put himself at such risk was surely crazy, his enemies had to wonder what else such an unstable person might do.

Whatever terrible deeds Blackbeard did carry out, he was at least at times a man of his word. It is easy to explain why he released some of the hostages he had taken from the colony of North Carolina. If he had simply killed everyone he captured at this time, he would have had no bargaining power with Governor Eden. But if he was the treacherous murderer many stories claim him to have been, why did he honor his agreement and free the remaining hostages after he received the medical supplies he demanded? One may argue that he was laying the groundwork for his supposed business arrangement with Eden. But this relationship too has never been proven.

Many of the best stories include both heroes and villains. This may be why history has been so harsh with Charles Eden and so kind to Alexander Spotswood. It is easy to label Eden as an **accomplice**—it makes the tale more interesting. But there is more evidence to support Spotswood's criminal character than Eden's. Perhaps over time the stories have molded themselves in favor of interesting characters over truthful accounts. History tells us that Governor Spotswood was removed from office in

A statue of Blackbeard stands at Blackbeard Castle on the island of St. Thomas—now part of the U.S. Virgin Islands.

1722. But even this dishonorable end did little to tarnish his hero's status in the tales about Blackbeard.

Stories about Blackbeard, including ghost tales, persist to this day. Some residents of North Carolina's Outer Banks claim to have seen Blackbeard's body swimming in the Atlantic where it is still searching for his severed head. Others say Blackbeard's ghost appears when someone gets too close to his buried treasure. While the stories themselves may be mere inventions, their staying power has only added to the long-dead pirate's aura.

They have also strengthened the belief in Blackbeard's treasure. If it does exist, it would be worth a fortune in more ways than one. Gold and silver are, of course, valuable in their own right. But belonging to the famed pirate would only make the metal more precious in the eyes of buyers. Alas, writes Abigail Tucker, "Except for a sprinkling of gold dust—less than one ounce so far—no treasure has been found aboard the vessel likely piloted by Edward Teach . . ."[2]

For archeologists, the wreckage recovered from Blackbeard's ship is treasure indeed. In October 2011, an eight-foot cannon was raised from the Atlantic floor off North Carolina.

National Geographic isn't hopeful that a treasure chest hidden by Blackbeard lies waiting to be uncovered. "Sadly, buried treasures—and the ubiquitous treasure maps—are also largely a myth."[3] History has shown us that pirates weren't concerned with planning for the future. Instead, they spent their ill-gotten money foolishly and quickly.

Writers love tales of ghosts and treasure. Even if you don't believe them, it's easy to get caught up in the legends, which have taken on a life of their own. After visiting the Outer Banks of North Carolina, Joseph Cosco shares that "If Blackbeard's treasure exists, it's in the countless shops and other businesses that capitalize on the Blackbeard and pirate theme." While the pirate is long gone, his name is definitely still making money—this time, legally. Still, Cosco favors the stories over the merchandise. "I prefer to see Blackbeard's treasure in the legends that survive in North Carolina's Blackbeard country. They are a fitting legacy for America's most popular **buccaneer**."[4]

Chapter Notes

Chapter 1: The Most Feared Pirate

1. Benjamin Barker, *Blackbeard*. Boston: F. Gleason, 1847, p. 3.

2. Benjamin Barker, *Blackbeard*. Boston: F. Gleason, 1847, p. 10.

3. Colin Woodard, "The Last Days of Blackbeard." Smithsonian.com, February 2014.
http://www.smithsonianmag.com/history/
last-days-blackbeard-180949440/?all

4. _____, "Friday Interview: Exposing Myths About Blackbeard the Pirate." *Carolina Journal Online*, April 19, 2013.
http://www.carolinajournal.com/exclusives/display_exclusive.
html?id=10073

5. Colin Woodard, "The Last Days of Blackbeard." Smithsonian.com, February 2014.
http://www.smithsonianmag.com/history/
last-days-blackbeard-180949440/?all

Chapter 2: From Privateering to Piracy

1. Carl Goerch, *Ocracoke*. Winston-Salem, NC: John F. Blair, 1956, p. 188.

2. Ibid.

3. Ibid.

4. Brian Hicks, "Blackbeard a local?; Books claims pirate from Goose Creek." *The Post and Courier*, December 5, 2011.

5. Ibid.

Chapter 3: Working Together

1. Stefan Lovgren, "Grim Life Cursed Real Pirates of Caribbean." *National Geographic News*, July 11, 2003.
http://news.nationalgeographic.com/
news/2003/07/0711_030711_piratescarribean_2.html

2. North Carolina Historic Sites, Historic Bath: Blackbeard the Pirate.
http://www.nchistoricsites.org/bath/blackbeard.htm

3. Ibid.

4. Ibid.

Chapter 4: Governor Spotswood to the Rescue

1. Mark St. John Erickson, "TODAY: VIRGINIA GOES ON HUNT FOR BLACKBEARD." *Daily Press*, May 27, 2012.

2. Gregory Elder, "Blackbeard: A sinner on the high seas." *Redland Daily Facts*, March 3, 2010.

3. Ibid.

4. Colin Woodard, "The Last Days of Blackbeard." Smithsonian.com, February 2014.

http://www.smithsonianmag.com/history/last-days-blackbeard-180949440/?all

5. Ibid.

6. Ibid.

Chapter 5: Buried Treasure

1. Joseph Cosco, "Blackbeard's Lair; The 18th-Century Pirate's Path in North Carolina." *The Washington Post*, November 28, 1993.

2. Ibid.

3. Ibid.

4. Ibid.

5. Abigail Tucker, "Did Archeologists Uncover Blackbeard's Treasure?" Smithsonian.com, March 2011.

http://www.smithsonianmag.com/history/did-archaeologists-uncover-blackbeards-treasure-215890/?no-ist

6. Jeremy A. Kaplan, "Off the North Carolina coast, pirate treasure of a different sort." Fox News, August 14, 2013.

http://www.foxnews.com/science/2013/08/14/off-north-carolina-coast-pirate-treasure-different-sort/

Chapter 6: The Truth Within the Legend

1. Stefan Lovgren, "Grim Life Cursed Real Pirates of Caribbean." *National Geographic News*, July 11, 2003.

http://news.nationalgeographic.com/news/2003/07/0711_030711_piratescarribean_2.html

2. Abigail, Tucker, "Did Archeologists Uncover Blackbeard's Treasure?" Smithsonian.com, March 2011.

http://www.smithsonianmag.com/history/did-archaeologists-uncover-blackbeards-treasure-215890/?no-ist

3. Joseph Cosco, "Blackbeard's Lair; The 18th-Century Pirate's Path in North Carolina." *The Washington Post*, November 28, 1993.

4. Ibid.

Works Consulted

Barker, Benjamin. *Blackbeard*. Boston: F. Gleason, 1847.

Cordingly, David. *Under the Black Flag*. New York: Random House, 1996.

Defoe, Danie . *A General History of the Pyrates*. (Edited by Manuel Schonhorn). Mineola, NY: Dover Publications, 1999.

Elder, Gregory. "Blackbeard: A sinner on the high seas." *Redland Daily Facts*, March 3, 2010.

Erickson, Mark St. John. "TODAY: VIRGINIA GOES ON HUNT FOR BLACKBEARD." *Daily Press*, May 27, 2012.

Goerch, Carl. *Ocracoke*. Winston-Salem, NC: John F. Blair, 1956.

Hicks, Brian. "Blackbeard a local?; Books claims pirate from Goose Creek." *The Post and Courier*, December 5, 2011.

Hudson, Christopher. "BLACKBEARDS LAST SECRET; His blood-curling antics and satanic appearance terrified even his own men. Now the discovery of a pewter syringe in a shipwreck may finally explain his murderous madness..." *Daily Mail*, November 10, 2006.

Konstam, Angus. *Blackbeard: America's Most Notorious Pirate*. Hoboken, NJ, John Wiley and Sons, 2006.

Konstam, Angus. *The World Atlas of Pirates*. Guilford, CT: the Lyons Press, 2009.

Millard, Candice. "The real pirates of the Caribbean." *International Herald Tribune*, June 2, 2007.

Woodard, Colin. *The Republic of Pirates: Being the True and Surprising Story of the Caribbean Pirates and the Man Who Brought Them Down*. New York: Mariner Books, 2008.

Further Reading

_____, *Blackbeard: The Life and Legacy of History's Most Famous Pirate*. Boston: Charles River Editors, 2012.

Croce, Pat. *Blackbeard*. Philadelphia: Running Press Kids, 2011.

Konstam, Angus. *Blackbeard's Last Fight—Pirate Hunting in North Carolina 1718*. Oxford, UK: Osprey Publlishing, 2013.

On the Internet

_____, "Friday Interview: Exposing Myths About Blackbeard the Pirate." Beaufort County Now, April 21, 2013.

http://beaufortcountynow.com/post/7162/friday-interview-exposing-myths-about-blackbeard-the-pirate.html

Hudson, Christopher. "The Real Jack Sparrow: He would have eaten Johnny Depp for breakfast." *The Daily Mail*, May 26, 2007.

http://www.dailymail.co.uk/femail/article-457724/The-Real-Jack-Sparrow-He-eaten-Johnny-Depp-breakfast.html

Kaplan, Jeremy A. "Off the North Carolina coast, pirate treasure of a different sort." Fox News, August 14, 2013.

http://www.foxnews.com/science/2013/08/14/off-north-carolina-coast-pirate-treasure-different-sort/

Lovgren, Stefan. "Grim Life Cursed Real Pirates of Caribbean." *National Geographic News*, July 11, 2003.

http://news.nationalgeographic.com/news/2003/07/0711_030711_piratescarribean.html

National Geographic, Blackbeard—Pirate Terror at Sea.

http://www.nationalgeographic.com/pirates/bbeard.html

North Carolina Historic Sites, Historic Bath: Blackbeard the Pirate

http://www.nchistoricsites.org/bath/blackbeard.htm

North Carolina History Project, The Pirate Blackbeard

http://www.northcarolinahistory.org/encyclopedia/466/entry

Tucker, Abigail. "Did Archeologists Uncover Blackbeard's Treasure?" Smithsonian.com, March 2011.

http://www.smithsonianmag.com/history/did-archaeologists-uncover-blackbeards-treasure-215890/?no-ist

Woodard, Colin. "The Last Days of Blackbeard." Smithsonian.com, February 2014.

http://www.smithsonianmag.com/history/last-days-blackbeard-180949440/?all

Glossary

accomplice (uh-KOM-plis)—one associated with another in wrongdoing

ambush (AM-boosh)—to attack by surprise

buccaneer (buhk-uh-NEER) pirates who raided Spanish colonies and ships along the American coast

civilized (SIV-uh-lahyzd)—raised out of a primitive state; advanced in social development

flog (FLAWG)—to beat severely with or as if with a rod or whip

galleon (GAL-ee-uh n) —a large sailing vessel used as a merchant ship

hostage (HOS-tij)—a person held captive as a pledge that promises will be kept or terms met by another

lair (LAIR)—a refuge or hideaway

letter of marque and reprisal (LET-er uv MARK and ree-PRIZ-l): A letter from a king or other ruler giving permission for a sea captain to attack an enemy.

maroon (muh-ROON))—to put ashore and abandon on a lonely island or coast

plunder (PLUHN-der)—to rob especially openly and by force (as in a raid)

privateer (prahy-vuh-TEER)—a sailor on an armed private ship permitted by its government to make war on ships of an enemy country

preposterous (pri-POS-ter-uhs)—making little or no sense

protégé [proh-tuh-ZHEY] French, a person under the care of someone interested in his or her career

stiletto (sti-LET-oh)—a slender dagger

swashbuckler (SWOSH-buhk-ler)—a swaggering or daring soldier or adventurer

trove (TROHV)—treasure of unknown ownership found buried or hidden

Index

About the Author

Tammy Gagne is the author of numerous books for adults and children, including *Caribbean Cultures in Perspective* and *The Evolution of Government and Politics: Venezuela* for Mitchell Lane Publishers. She resides in northern New England with her husband and son. One of her favorite pastimes is visiting schools to speak to kids about the writing process.